MW01283924

Made in the USA
Columbia, SC
16 October 2023

24537651R00074